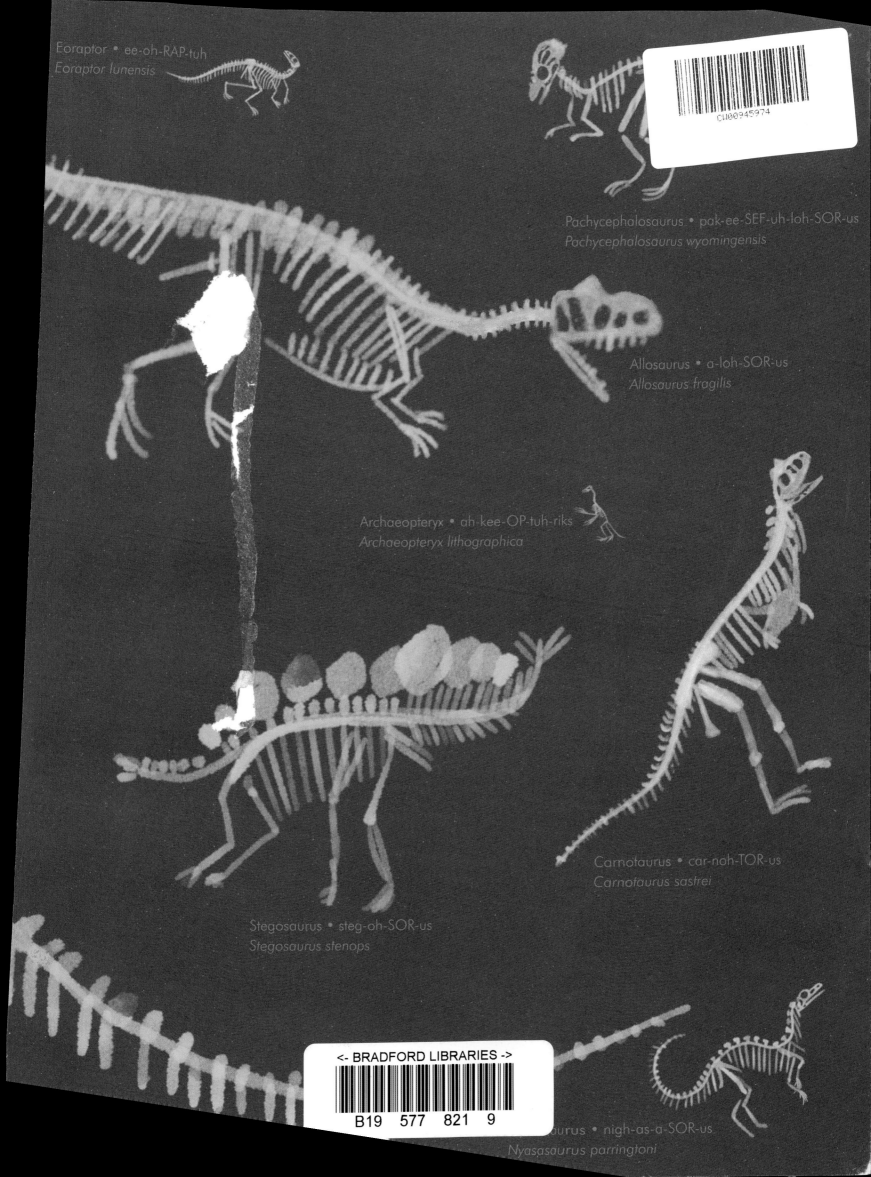

Eoraptor • ee-oh-RAP-tuh
Eoraptor lunensis

Pachycephalosaurus • pak-ee-SEF-uh-loh-SOR-us
Pachycephalosaurus wyomingensis

Allosaurus • a-loh-SOR-us
Allosaurus fragilis

Archaeopteryx • ah-kee-OP-tuh-riks
Archaeopteryx lithographica

Stegosaurus • steg-oh-SOR-us
Stegosaurus stenops

Carnotaurus • car-noh-TOR-us
Carnotaurus sastrei

...aurus • nigh-as-a-SOR-us
Nyasasaurus parringtoni

AN ADVENTURER'S GUIDE TO DINOSAURS

WRITTEN BY
ISABEL THOMAS

FOREWORD BY
CHRIS PACKHAM

ILLUSTRATED BY
YAS IMAMURA

LADYBIRD BOOKS

Ladybird Books is part of the Penguin Random House group
of companies whose addresses can be found
at global.penguinrandomhouse.com.
www.penguin.co.uk   www.puffin.co.uk   www.ladybird.co.uk

Penguin
Random House
UK

First published 2021
001
Foreword copyright © Chris Packham, 2021
Text by Isabel Thomas
Illustrations by Yas Imamura
Consultant: Robert Theodore
Text and illustrations copyright © Ladybird Books Ltd, 2021
Printed in China
The authorized representative in the EEA is Penguin Random House Ireland,
Morrison Chambers, 32 Nassau Street, Dublin D02 YH68
A CIP catalogue record for this book is available from the British Library
ISBN: 978–0–241–47189–0
All correspondence to:
Ladybird Books, Penguin Random House Children's
One Embassy Gardens, 8 Viaduct Gardens
London SW11 7BW

This book contains a Dinosaur Adventure on every spread!
These interactive activities should be carried out safely with support
from an adult and plenty of space to move around.

CONTENTS

BOARDING PASS

Foreword

I loved dinosaurs when I was five, and I still love dinosaurs now.

Why is that, I wonder? I think it's because some dinosaurs were very big, and big can be impressive. Others were very fierce, and fierce is always exciting! But most importantly, they are all extinct.

I have always been able to imagine what dinosaurs were like, but what's really exciting is that I now imagine dinosaurs very differently than I did when I was five. This is because scientists have learnt more and more about dinosaurs throughout my lifetime. In some ways, what we know about dinosaurs has changed more in the last 50 years than in the previous 65 million!

So, what I now wonder is, what will we learn about dinosaurs in another 50 years? Maybe you might become a scientist and help find out. And I can't think of anything more exciting than finding out new things about dinosaurs!

Chris Packham

Finding fossils

Fossils are very special rocks. They show the shapes of plants and animals that lived millions of years ago, and they give us clues about what Earth was like before humans existed.

Today, lots of different animals live on Earth. There are reptiles and birds, insects and fish. Many of the largest animals are mammals. Millions of years ago, the only mammals were small and shy, and reptiles ruled the land, sky and sea.

One group of reptiles included animals so large and fearsome that scientists named them "terrible lizards". These were the dinosaurs.

Dinosaurs lived on Earth for more than 160 million years. That's 800 times longer than humans have been here!

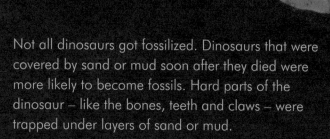

Not all dinosaurs got fossilized. Dinosaurs that were covered by sand or mud soon after they died were more likely to become fossils. Hard parts of the dinosaur – like the bones, teeth and claws – were trapped under layers of sand or mud.

Over a long time, the tiny pieces of sand or mud turned into rock. The trapped bones, teeth and claws were slowly replaced by rock, too. Fossils aren't the actual bones, teeth or claws of dinosaurs, but they show us their shape.

Dinosaur adventure

Close this book and put it down on a table. Look at it from the side, so you can see the edge of the pages. Imagine that the pages are all layers of rock. The oldest layers are the pages at the bottom of the book. The newest layers are at the top. This means that the dinosaur fossils we find in the deepest layers of rock are the oldest.

Some fossils show us what dinosaurs looked like. Fossils can also help us to work out what dinosaurs ate, how they moved and whether they roared, honked or squeaked!

The rock around a fossil helps us to work out when a dinosaur lived. It can give clues about what the environment was like then.

Most fossils are found in sedimentary rocks, which are rocks with lots of layers. The deepest layers are the oldest, so the deepest fossils must be the oldest, too.

Some fossils show the shape of dinosaur eggs and footprints.

Before the dinosaurs

To understand how dinosaurs came to rule the Earth, we need
to look back almost 300 million years to a time before the dinosaurs.
This part of history is called the Permian. It lasted around 50 million years.

Back then, the whole world was very different. Even the land was in different
places! Most land was grouped together in one enormous continent.
The rest of the planet was covered by a vast ocean.

Fossils show that there were lots of plants,
insects and reptiles in the Permian. But the
reptiles looked nothing like today's snakes
and lizards. They looked more like monsters!

There were no humans when the world
looked like this. The huge continent is
called Pangaea and the huge ocean
is called Panthalassa.

*Sauroctonus
progressus*

If you drew a dinosaur family tree
going back for millions of years, you
would find some Permian reptiles!

The world used to be warm, wet and swampy. Over millions of years, the climate changed a lot. By the Permian period, some parts of Pangaea were very hot and dry. It was too dry for animals like frogs. But reptiles with thick skin like living in hot, dry places.

Dinosaur adventure

Put this book on the floor and take 30 steps away from it. Each step is 10 million years. Turn around and take five steps back towards the book. You have just walked through the Permian! Take another eighteen steps to walk through the age of the dinosaurs. Finally, there is a big gap of more than six steps. You have now reached the first humans.

Eorasaurus olsoni

Idelesaurus tataricus

At the end of the Permian, the world changed forever. Let's go and see what happened!

You would find some Permian reptiles if you drew a family tree for today's mammals! These Permian reptiles were called therapsids. Some therapsids could heat their own bodies, just like humans. This meant they could live in places where the temperature changed a lot from day to night, and from summer to winter.

Dvinosaurus primus

CRETACEOUS

The Triassic

Rocks from the Permian contain many different types of fossils. Earth was full of life! But when we look inside rocks that formed just after the Permian, there are very few fossils to be found.

This shows that about 252 million years ago, just before the Triassic, most of the animals on Earth suddenly became extinct. We call this the Great Dying.

Some scientists think the Great Dying happened because lots of volcanoes erupted, and the smoke and ash blocked out the sun. Without sunlight, the plants would have died and left the animals with nothing to eat.

Others think it was because the climate changed quickly, and the world became too warm for most animals to live.

Garjainia prima

Just one in ten Permian species survived the Great Dying. Animals that survived had all the food, water and shelter on the planet to themselves. The ancestors of dinosaurs began to develop. New and bigger creatures appeared. This was the start of the Triassic.

PERMIAN	TRIASSIC 201 to 251 millions of years before today		JURASSIC

Dinosaur adventure

Hold this book in one hand. Move the book around, pretending it is *Garjainia prima*'s heavy head and your wrist is its neck. Your wrist muscles will quickly get tired! There are no fossils of muscles, because only hard parts like bones and teeth get fossilized. But *Garjainia prima* must have had a very strong, muscly neck to move its huge head about.

Lystrosaurus had two tiny tusks, and a beak for biting leaves off plants. This was no defence against a hungry meat eater!

**Lystrosaurus
georgi**

I recognize a few of these creatures from the Permian, but there are some amazing new animals, too! They are the first archosaurs. Let's go further into the Triassic to find out more.

Garjainia prima was one of a group of reptiles called erythrosuchids. It was about the size of a lion, with a huge head and a powerful bite. Like today's lions, it hunted herbivores, which are animals that eat plants.

CRETACEOUS

The first dinosaurs

Lots of new archosaurs appeared in the Triassic. The archosaurs were a large group of reptiles. They included flying reptiles, ancient crocodiles and the very first dinosaurs.

Archosaurs means "ruling reptiles". It's a good name for these creatures because, during the Triassic, the archosaurs began to take over the world!

Some of the archosaurs had legs that stuck out from the sides of their bodies – like crocodiles and lizards today. This made it hard to walk, so they moved slowly. Dinosaurs were different. Their legs and feet were right underneath their bodies. This helps scientists to work out if a fossil is from a dinosaur or another kind of archosaur.

We've travelled to the middle of the Triassic, to a part of the world that is now Tanzania. This archosaur is one of the very first dinosaurs!

Stenaulorhynchus stockleyi

The first dinosaurs were small and fast. They were probably omnivores, which means that they ate plants and other animals.

Dinosaur adventure

Look closely at the *Nyasasaurus*'s hands. Think of all the different ways you use your own hands. Dinosaurs didn't have thumbs like we do, but their hands may still have given them a big advantage over their Triassic rivals.

Rhamphorhynchoidea

Nyasasaurus was about the size of a kangaroo, with long legs and a long neck. It may have walked on its two back legs and used its hands to grab food.

Nyasasaurus parringtoni

The oldest dinosaur fossils ever found are from a *Nyasasaurus*. The fossils were discovered in rocks that are about 243 million years old.

The *Nyasasaurus* fossils found by scientists include part of an arm and some bones from its spine. These bones have lots in common with the bones of other dinosaurs, which tells scientists that *Nyasasaurus* was a dinosaur, too. One big clue is that its bones grew quickly, like lots of dinosaurs' bones. Scientists have used what we already know about other dinosaurs to work out what *Nyasasaurus* looked like.

Different diets

Fossils of the first dinosaurs look quite similar to one another, but fossils from later in the Triassic are much more varied. By then, dinosaurs were different sizes, and had different ways of moving about and finding food.

Scientists use lots of clues to work out what dinosaurs ate. Sometimes, fossils of other plants and animals are discovered near a dinosaur fossil. Other times, there are even fossils of dinosaur dung, called coprolites! These can be full of the crunched-up fossils of smaller animals and plants.

*Herrerasaurus
ischigualastensis*

This dinosaur also had long fingers with claws for grabbing its prey so it didn't get away! These clues tell us that *Herrerasaurus* was a carnivore, which is an animal that only eats meat.

Roar! A dinosaur's fossilized teeth are clues about what the dinosaur liked to eat!

Dinosaur adventure

Although today we think of all dinosaurs as being really big, *Eoraptor* was only about as tall as a chicken! And from nose to tail, it was just over three times as long as this book. Lie on the floor and use the longest edge of the book to help you work out the length of an *Eoraptor*. Are you bigger than it was?

Herrerasaurus had very unusual teeth. They were all sharp and serrated for chomping through meat and bone.

Eoraptor had more than 100 teeth in its tiny mouth. It had small, sharp teeth for biting through meat and bone, but it also had larger teeth to grind up soft plants. Humans have different kinds of teeth, too. This is a clue that *Eoraptor* was an omnivore. Like us, it probably ate a mixture of plants and small animals.

**Eoraptor
lunensis**

Beastly feet

Fossilized dinosaur footprints can show how dinosaurs moved, and even how quickly they travelled!

In a quarry in New Mexico, USA, scientists have discovered thousands of Triassic fossils, including hundreds of *Coelophysis* skeletons. This dinosaur lived about 210 million years ago.

Coelophysis was one of the earliest dinosaurs in a group called the "beast-footed" dinosaurs, or theropods. In the Triassic, theropods were still quite small, but *Coelophysis* was already an expert at hunting and eating other animals. It had strong, serrated teeth that could crunch through meat and bone!

Later, the theropods would include huge carnivores like *Tyrannosaurus rex*.

We're near the end of the Triassic, in a part of the world that is now North America. Look at the footprints left in the mud by *Coelophysis*!

Coelophysis footprints tell us that it ran faster than the world's fastest humans! It used its speed to catch insects and small animals. The fossils of its prey have been found in the part of a *Coelophysis* skeleton that would have been its belly!

Coelophysis

By the end of the Triassic, all sorts of dinosaurs lived in many different habitats on land. They included small two-legged dinosaurs and some of the first larger dinosaurs that walked on four legs. Dinosaurs didn't rule the world yet, but once again everything was about to change.

Dinosaur adventure

The footprints on this page show what a life-sized *Coelophysis* footprint looked like. Take off your shoes and put your own foot carefully on the picture. Can you imagine how big a *Coelophysis* would be if it stood next to you?

The Jurassic

The Jurassic began 201 million years ago and lasted about 55 million years. Earth was changing quickly and dinosaurs were beginning to take over the world.

The Triassic ended the same way it began, with a mysterious extinction event. Up to 80% of the species on Earth died out in a short space of time. Most of the archosaurs became extinct, but dinosaurs, pterosaurs and crocodile-like reptiles survived. Their numbers grew and they moved to live in new places.

During the Jurassic, Earth changed in many ways, too. The huge continent of Pangaea broke apart into smaller continents that began to move away from each other. The weather became warmer and wetter.

There were two different groups of dinosaurs. Scientists tell them apart by the shape of the bones in their hips. They are known as "bird-hipped" and "lizard-hipped" dinosaurs.

Heterodontosaurus tucki

Like most early-Jurassic bird-hipped dinosaurs, *Heterodontosaurus* was small and walked on two legs. But its teeth were special. It had three different types – sharp biting teeth at the front for nibbling leaves, grinding teeth at the back for chewing plants and cone-shaped teeth that stuck out like tiny tusks.

TRIASSIC

JURASSIC 145 to 201
millions of years before today

Dinosaur adventure

Dinosaurs had long tails that helped them to balance. Try walking like a dinosaur. Bend your knees and lean forward. Hold this book in your hands and stretch your arms out in front of you, like a long neck. Try to walk – it's hard! Now bring the book behind you, holding it in both hands, like a tail. Try walking again. Is it easier?

Dinosaurs in the lizard-hipped group were beginning to get bigger. *Massospondylus* had a long neck and legs. It could reach plants that shorter herbivores couldn't.

Jurassic rocks contain fossils of hundreds of dinosaurs that aren't found in Triassic rocks. This shows that hundreds of new dinosaurs evolved in the Jurassic!

Massospondylus carinatus

Scientists have even found fossils of unhatched *Massospondylus* eggs. The baby dinosaurs had very large heads compared to their bodies, and they probably crawled along on four legs before they learned to walk on two!

CRETACEOUS

Showing off

In the Jurassic, theropod dinosaurs became the top predators. These meat-eating dinosaurs were much larger than the Triassic theropods.

Jurassic theropods moved surprisingly quickly on their two powerful legs and hunted other animals, including smaller dinosaurs. They had short arms and small hands.

Dilophosaurus had four fingers. Of these, it used two long clawed fingers and one shorter clawed finger to grasp its prey.

Dilophosaurus was one of the biggest carnivores of its time. It had lots of long, thin teeth like curved needles.

Dilophosaurus wetherilli

Dilophosaurus had a pair of crests on its head. We know the crests were hard and made of bone because they have been preserved as fossils. The crests might have helped *Dilophosaurus* to cool down, and it probably also used the crests like a peacock uses its tail — to show off to other dinosaurs!

Dilophosaurus was six metres long! If we took one home, it would just squeeze through the door, but it would need to sleep across four king-size beds!

Dilophosaurus footprints have been found in groups, so they may have worked together to catch prey.

The only mammal-like creatures to survive the Triassic were small – the size of cats, rats and mice. They ran around in the shadows, trying to stay hidden from the dinosaurs!

Kayentatherium wellesi

Dinosaur adventure

Open up this book so it forms a V-shape and hold it on top of your head. Pretend you are a *Dilophosaurus*, showing off your crests. Can you strut, pose and preen like a peacock?

Bigger bites

Meat-eating dinosaurs became bigger during the Jurassic – and so did their teeth!

Allosaurus was one of the most enormous Jurassic predators. It was about the length of a tennis net, but around five times as high, and it could run at around 30 kilometres per hour. That's roughly twice as fast as you would pedal on a bike! Heavy herbivores like *Stegosaurus* could not outrun *Allosaurus*, but they were good at standing their ground and fighting back.

Allosaurus fragilis

Allosaurus had serrated teeth that were up to 10 centimetres long. Their teeth curved backwards, which made it harder for prey to wriggle free, and regrew if they broke off.

Allosaurus lived for about 25 years, and became adults when they were fifteen.

Lots of *Allosaurus* fossils have marks that show the dinosaur had broken bones or damaged claws. One tail-bone fossil has a missing chunk that matches the shape of a *Stegosaurus* tail spike!

Woah! We've arrived in the middle of a fight between a carnivore and a herbivore. Let's keep quiet and watch.

Dinosaur adventure

Scientists have worked out how wide some dinosaurs would have been able to open their mouths, and *Allosaurus* was one of the widest. Trace these lines on to a piece of paper. Open up this book on the piece of paper, lining up the longest edges with the lines you've drawn. This is how wide *Allosaurus* could open its mouth. Compare it to how wide you can open your mouth – it's about one-and-a-half times as wide!

92°

Scientists have found a *Stegosaurus* plate fossil that looks like it has been bitten by an *Allosaurus*. That means *Allosaurus* teeth were tough enough to bite through bone!

Stegosaurus's strange plates puzzle scientists. Perhaps they helped these huge dinosaurs to cool down. Or perhaps they were brightly coloured to help *Stegosaurus* attract or scare away other dinosaurs!

Stegosaurus stenops

There were lots of different kinds of stegosaurs, but *Stegosaurus* was one of the largest. It was the size of a double-decker bus and weighed as much as today's rhinoceros.

Stegosaurus's plates weren't weapons, but the four long spikes on its tail probably were. Some fossils of these tail spikes have broken tips, where it looks like the bone has repaired itself after an injury.

23

Leafy giants

Giant plant-eating sauropods were the biggest dinosaurs of all. The first huge sauropods were stomping around the world by the Late Jurassic.

The sauropods were the largest land animals to have ever lived on Earth. These four-legged lizard-hipped dinosaurs could grow up to twice the height of today's giraffes. *Giraffatitan* was one of the biggest sauropods of the Jurassic. Its long neck made it as tall as a four-storey building, helping it to eat plants that no other dinosaur could reach.

Kentrosaurus aethiopicus

Sauropod fossils contain clues about how these big bodies actually worked. Like today's giraffes, the bones of the sauropods' long necks were full of small air pockets, like honeycomb, which made them light but strong.

Giraffatitan's nostrils were right on top of its snout, so it didn't even have to take a break from eating to breathe!

24

Giraffatitan was much bigger than any meat-eating dinosaur. This probably helped to keep it safe. Some scientists think that one group of sauropods, the diplodocids, may have used their long tails for defence, too. They might have used them to knock predators off their feet, or whipped them to make a booming noise to scare predators away!

Dinosaur adventure

Put this book down at one end of a long hallway, or in a park or garden. Carefully flip the book over as shown. Repeat this 27 times and you'll have measured out the length of a *Giraffatitan*'s neck. If you have space, flip the book over another 44 times. Now you will have travelled all the way to the tip of *Giraffatitan*'s tail!

There were no plants with flowers, fruits or nuts in the Jurassic. Sauropods like *Giraffatitan* ate fir trees, ferns and strange-looking plants called horsetails. Like today's zebras and wildebeests, sauropods would have spent all day grazing, because horsetails contain a similar amount of energy to grass.

Giraffatitan didn't have chewing teeth – it just tore off leaves and twigs and swallowed them whole. Food in its stomach would slowly be broken down by microbes, just like grass in a cow's stomach. For *Giraffatitan*, this could take up to two weeks!

African elephants are now the biggest land animals on Earth, and they eat for about eighteen hours a day. Sauropods were much bigger. They must have guzzled a lot of food to grow so big! Their long necks were the secret to their success. Just by reaching around they could eat for hours without taking a step, which would have saved them a lot of energy.

25

Feathers and fuzz

People used to think that all dinosaurs had smooth, scaly skin, like reptiles today. Now, we've found clues to suggest that many dinosaurs were actually fuzzy!

Most fossils are formed from the hard parts of an animal, such as bones, horns and teeth. That's why museums often contain fossilized dinosaur skeletons. At first, this meant scientists had to guess what dinosaurs looked like. Over time, they've found fossils formed by the softer bits of dinosaurs, such as skin, scales and feathers.

Kulindadromeus was only a little dinosaur – about the size of a turkey – but sometimes the smallest fossils reveal the biggest surprises! Some of the oldest dinosaur fossils with signs of a fuzzy coating are *Kulindadromeus*.

We know that *Kulindadromeus* lived near active volcanoes, because there is ash in the rock around its fossils!

Ash from the volcanoes buried *Kulindadromeus* quickly when it died. This helped to preserve its fuzzy coating.

Kulindadromeus's fuzzy coat might have helped to keep it warm by trapping heat, like the fur and feathers of today's mammals and birds.

Kulindadromeus had a mixture of different kinds of fuzz. It had fluffy legs and arms, a bit like down on today's baby birds, and short, stiff bristles on its head and body. Only its feet and tail were scaly.

Kulindadromeus zabaikalicus

Dinosaur adventure

Look at the different parts of *Kulindadromeus*'s body in the picture. Can you think of any animals alive today that have different amounts of fur or feathers on different parts of their bodies? How might this help them to survive?

Winged reptiles

Pterosaurs are the most famous winged archosaurs, but some small dinosaurs had wings, too!

Archaeopteryx was a small Jurassic animal, about the size of a raven. When it was first discovered, scientists thought it was one of the very first birds, but birds don't have teeth, long, bony tails or claws at the ends of their wings! *Archaeopteryx* was actually a small theropod dinosaur.

The ancestors of today's birds were theropod dinosaurs!

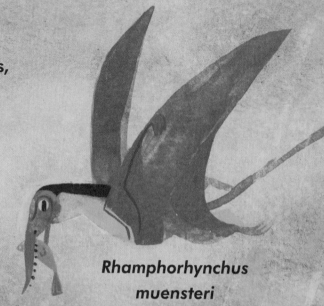

Rhamphorhynchus muensteri

Compsognathus longipes

Compsognathus was a theropod, too. It was about the size of a chicken, with simple feathers but no wings. Its long tail helped it to change direction very quickly when it was running to catch small, fast prey, such as lizards.

In the Jurassic, it was often sunny and warm but there were tropical storms, too! During the storms, land animals and plants would be washed into lakes. Eventually, some of them became fossils.

Pterosaurs could fly for long distances and swoop down from the sky to grab prey with their beaks!

Pterosaurs were not dinosaurs, but they were in the same big group of reptiles – the archosaurs. Pterosaurs had wings made of skin and muscle that stretched between their back legs and their long fingers. When they were on the ground, they folded their wings and used them like front legs.

Archaeopteryx had long, feathered wings, but we don't know if it could fly. It might have just flapped its wings to glide short distances to get away from predators!

Archaeopteryx
lithographica

Dinosaur adventure

Archaeopteryx fossils are found in Germany, in a type of sedimentary rock called Solnhofen Limestone. Scientists have found fossils from more than 750 different plants and animals in the same rocks. Can you spot these animals in the picture? Remember, they lived about 155 million years ago, so they look a little different from their relatives alive today.

- ammonite
- fish
- crab
- dragonfly
- lobster
- jellyfish

The Cretaceous

The Cretaceous was a period of Earth's history that began 145 million years ago. Dinosaurs filled the land and skies, and even bigger reptiles ruled the seas.

During the Cretaceous, the world was bursting with new types of plants and animals. On land, the dinosaurs were still in charge. Many new types of dinosaur appeared, too!

Caudipteryx was a birdlike theropod that lived in a part of the world that is now China. It was covered in short, fluffy feathers. It had longer feathers on its arms and a fan of feathers at the end of its tail. It probably used its feathers for showing off or for keeping its eggs warm.

Confuciusornis
sanctus

Caudipteryx zoui

All these winged dinosaurs shared the skies with some of the world's very first birds, such as *Confuciusornis*!

Some small theropods had the right kind of feathers for flying. *Microraptor* had long feathers on its legs and arms. It may have been able to fly, or at least steer while gliding.

Microraptor gui

PERMIAN	TRIASSIC		JURASSIC

Confuciusornis was the first bird to have a beak.

Dinosaur adventure

Find a piece of chalk or a chalky rock and draw one of the creatures you see on this page. Most chalky rocks that we dig up today were formed in the Cretaceous, from the shells of tiny sea creatures. When you use chalk, you are holding the fossils of thousands of Cretaceous creatures!

Fossils from much larger Cretaceous theropods have also been found in China, including *Yutyrannus* – a fluffy relative of *Tyrannosaurus rex*!

Yutyrannus huali

Changyuraptor yangi

The Cretaceous lasted for 79 million years. That's nearly 400 times as long as humans have lived on Earth. During this vast stretch of time, Earth's land slowly split into smaller continents. Some were separated by shallow seas, others by deep oceans.

This four-winged *Changyuraptor* was a type of raptor. Raptors were close relatives of the first birds on Earth. Some of the feathers on its tail, arms and legs were as long as a classroom ruler! These are the longest feathers ever found on a dinosaur fossil.

CRETACEOUS 65 to 145
millions of years before today

Plant-eaters' paradise

The climate in the Cretaceous was different from place to place, just as it is today. But overall, the world was almost the warmest it has ever been. Places as far north as France today had a tropical climate. The North and South Poles were not covered in ice. Even Antarctica was home to animals – including dinosaurs!

Dinosaurs shaped like *Iguanodon* started to appear in the Late Jurassic. In the Cretaceous they grew in number and spread to almost every part of the world.

**Demandasaurus
darwini**

Montsechia was one of the first plants to have flowers! Plants with flowers began to appear during the Cretaceous, giving herbivores new types of food. Nectar, fruits and nuts are all packed with energy.

Dinosaur adventure

Put your hand next to *Iguanodon's* hand and look closely at the thumbs. If you had a thumb spike, what could you use it for?

Europejara olcadesorum

Fossils of dinosaurs like *Iguanodon* have been found together, in groups. This tells us that they may have lived together, like herds of goats and sheep today.

Some of the very first dinosaur fossils ever discovered by scientists were teeth from a giant herbivore just like this *Iguanodon*. They were similar to an iguana's teeth today, but much, MUCH bigger.

Iguanodon had four fingers and a thumb on each hand, and they each had different jobs. Three of the fingers had nails shaped like hooves, so *Iguanodon* could walk on its front legs. Its thumbs had giant spikes that may have helped the dinosaur to strip leaves from branches or crack open seeds.

Iguanodon bernissartensis

Sharper teeth and bigger claws

The biggest meat-eating dinosaurs lived during the Cretaceous. They evolved different kinds of teeth and claws, adapted to hunt and eat different kinds of prey.

Spinosaurus was the longest meat-eating dinosaur that ever lived. It had a long snout, like a crocodile's, lined with skewer-like teeth. It was brilliant at catching fish.

The rivers where *Spinosaurus* hunted were home to giant fish the size of basking sharks. Scientists have found many *Spinosaurus* teeth with spikes from the fish still stuck in them.

Today, North Africa is a hot, dry part of the world, but 90 million years ago it was home to massive mangrove forests flooded with seawater.

These teeth might look like a shark's, but they actually belong to a giant *Carcharodontosaurus saharicus*. This predator was up to 3 metres longer than *Tyrannosaurus rex* and had 15-centimetre-long teeth that could bite through tough skin.

Carcharodontosaurus may have stolen food from *Spinosaurus*!

Dinosaur adventure

Plant-eating dinosaurs had eyes on the sides of their heads. This helped them to spot predators sneaking up from the side or behind. Meat-eating theropods, like *Spinosaurus*, had eyes that faced forward instead. This helped them to grab prey. Human eyes work like *Spinosaurus*'s! Ask a friend to stand back from this book, cover one eye and use their pointed finger to touch the *Spinosaurus*'s eye on this page. Did they miss the first time? Humans use forward-facing eyes to help us judge distances correctly the first time.

Spinosaurus was named after the tall, bony spines that stick up from its backbone. When *Spinosaurus* was alive, its skin would have stretched between these spines, forming a huge sail.

Spinosaurus aegyptiacus

Dinosaurs didn't brush their teeth, so just one bite could leave behind nasty germs that could kill even a giant sauropod.

Spinosaurus's long, curved claws would have helped it to grip slippery fish.

Duck-billed dinosaurs

Duck-billed dinosaurs, or hadrosaurs, are known as "the cows of the Cretaceous" because they spent so much time grazing in herds! They had fancy crests on their heads.

The hadrosaurs are relatives of dinosaurs like *Iguanodon*. They are nicknamed "duck-billed" because of their skulls, which are shaped like a duck's head with a bill. Inside the bill-shaped snout is a huge, hollow nostril.

Parasaurolophus walkeri

Parasaurolophus had one of the largest head crests. Its nostrils looped all the way through its crest, opening out into different hollow spaces. Scientists have wondered if *Parasaurolophus* used its crest like a snorkel or air tank to breathe underwater, or maybe to warm the air it breathed in. It's likely the crest did the same job as the tubes in a trumpet or trombone – making the dinosaur's calls louder and deeper.

Having a loud call would have been very helpful for herd animals. It might have helped them find each other, or warn each other when a predator was nearby!

Sssh, look! Baby *Maiasaura*! They are only about 35 centimetres long when they hatch. They will stay safe in the nest, where their parent brings them food.

Maiasaura were hadrosaurs, too. Fossils from younger and older *Maiasaura* have been found next to each other, as well as nests full of hatched eggs. This gives us clues about how these dinosaur parents might have looked after their babies!

In the Late Cretaceous, hadrosaurs roamed all over in huge herds.

Maiasaura were the first dinosaurs in space! In 1985, an astronaut took *Maiasaura* fossils from Earth to a space station and back again.

Maiasaura peeblesorum

Dinosaur adventure

Have you ever put your hand into a pile of fallen leaves? As dead leaves rot, they release heat. *Maiasaura* piled leaves and plants on top of their eggs to keep them warm. This might sound strange, but crocodiles still do it today!

Maiasaura gathered together in big groups to build their nests in different areas to where they normally lived, just like many birds do today.

Dino defences

Heavy herbivores couldn't outrun the biggest meat-eating dinosaurs, but they had spectacular defences to help them stand their ground. Some dinosaurs had skin with built-in armour! This helped to shield them from the teeth and claws of giant predators.

Ankylosaurs are closely related to stegosaurs, but they had much better armour. Some animals have armour that sits on top of their skin, like the scales of a pangolin. But the bony plates and spikes of the ankylosaur grew inside its skin! Today's crocodiles have the same kind of protection.

Ankylosaurus was one of the biggest armoured dinosaurs. It had a wide body that was very close to the ground, like a tank. The top and sides of its body were covered in bony plates. It even had thin, bony plates inside its eyelids!

Ankylosaurus had a heavy, bony club at the end of its tail. By swinging this side-to-side, an *Ankylosaurus* could have knocked a predator like *Albertosaurus* right off its feet!

Ankylosaurus magniventris

Dinosaur adventure

Some of *Ankylosaurus*'s bony plates were about as thick as this book! Put the book on your lap, like a plate of armour, and knock on it. Can you feel how armour soaks up the energy of the knocking, so it doesn't reach your skin underneath?

Pachycephalosaurus
wyomingensis

The bony dome on *Pachycephalosaurus*'s head looked a bit like a crash helmet. Scientists think the dome might have helped these dinosaurs to recognize each other and tell who was strongest – a bit like a lion's mane!

This ankylosaur is called *Edmontonia*. It didn't have a tail club, but it did have sharp spikes along each side of its body and tail.

Albertosaurus was a type of tyrannosaur. It was shorter and lighter than *Tyrannosaurus rex*, but it had the same sharp, serrated teeth to grip its prey and tear off chunks of meat.

The biggest dinosaurs

By the end of the Cretaceous, dinosaurs were roaming around every continent on Earth. Some of them were the largest dinosaurs that ever lived – the titanosaurs.

Titanosaurs were gigantic sauropod dinosaurs. The biggest lived towards the end of the Cretaceous, in the southern part of the world. They were almost as big as blue whales! They walked on four sturdy legs to support their heavy bodies. Just like the Late Jurassic sauropods, they had hollow spaces in the bones in their backs to make them lighter.

Carnotaurus was a speedy meat-eating theropod that lived in the part of the world that is now Argentina. Its tail had powerful muscles along each side, which helped it to sprint very fast after prey. However, it probably wasn't very good at changing direction to avoid the sweeping tail of a sauropod!

Carnotaurus sastrei

Strangest of all were *Carnotaurus*'s arms, which were so tiny they likely did nothing at all! They were a feature left over from its ancestors, just as humans still have tiny tailbones that we don't need or use, left over from our ancestors who had tails.

Dinosaur adventure

See for yourself how long *Dreadnoughtus's* neck was. Find a long, open space. Put this book down at one end and mark the starting place. Flip the book over 35 times and mark the finishing place. You have travelled 11 metres! Imagine your head being that far away from the rest of your body. How would you scratch an itchy nose?

This part of the world lies in South America today. Sixty-six million years ago, it was home to the biggest dinosaurs of all!

Dreadnoughtus was one of the largest dinosaurs we know about.

Argentinosaurus huinculensis

Some sauropods, like *Dreadnoughtus*, used their long necks to reach leaves on tall trees. Others held their heads close to the ground, moving their necks to eat plants across a huge area of ground without taking a step.

We have only found thirteen bones from *Argentinosaurus*, but they show us it may have been even longer and taller than *Dreadnoughtus*! Scientists have estimated that *Argentinosaurus* was as long as eight cars and weighed almost as much as a blue whale.

Dreadnoughtus used its neck to reach leaves on high branches. Its neck was 11 metres long – that's about a hundred times as long as a human neck!

Dreadnoughtus schrani

Huge horns

As carnivores (and their teeth) became bigger, their prey adapted, too. Fossils show that Cretaceous herbivores had some of the most impressive dinosaur defences.

These dinosaurs also had frills, but not the kind of frills you find on fancy clothes! They may have been covered in keratin, the same material that makes horns and beaks hard.

Triceratops was about the size of an African elephant, making it one of the largest horned dinosaurs. Its horns were a metre long, and probably came in handy for self-defence. A fossilized *Triceratops* horn has been found with bite marks from *Tyrannosaurus rex* teeth!

Some fossilized frills contain holes made by other dinosaurs' horns. This is a big clue that *Triceratops* probably used their horns to fight each other, like many of today's horned animals do.

Triceratops horridus

Horned dinosaurs couldn't stand on their back legs to reach the leaves on trees. Instead, their tough beaks and grinding teeth helped them to eat woody shrubs that other herbivores couldn't chew through.

We've discovered fossils from more than 40 different kinds of horned dinosaurs.

A thick tail helped to balance the weight of *Tyrannosaurus*'s massive head.

Dinosaur adventure

As a *Triceratops* got older, its horns became longer and more twisted. When they reached over 1 metre long, they would have weighed almost 40 times as much as this book. Feel the weight of this book in your hands. What do you think it would feel like to carry such heavy horns on your face?

Dakotaraptor steini

Tyrannosaurus rex

Tyrannosaurus rex means "tyrant lizard king". The shapes inside fossils of their skulls tell us that *Tyrannosaurus* had a big brain for a dinosaur, with good hearing, great eyesight and a strong sense of smell. Serrated teeth the size of bananas also helped to make it a terrifyingly good hunter.

Tyrannosaurus was probably too heavy to sprint, but it didn't need to. Its powerful back legs helped it to walk about as fast as you can run!

43

What happened next?

At the end of the Cretaceous, another huge extinction event changed life on Earth forever. This time, the dinosaurs did not survive.

Inside rocks that are 66 million years old, there are fossils from hundreds of different Cretaceous plants and animals. But if we look inside rocks that are 65 million years old, most of these plants and animals have vanished. This tells us that around 66 million years ago, three-quarters of the plants and animals on Earth suddenly became extinct.

Scientists have found lots of clues that a giant meteorite crashed into Earth. This would have caused forest fires and flooding. It would have thrown dust and gases into the atmosphere, blocking the sun's light for several months.

Plants need sunlight to make food, so many plants would have died without it. Animals need to eat plants (or to eat animals that have eaten plants), so they would have died, too. Dinosaurs, pterosaurs and many marine animals became extinct.

Hainina

Some small Cretaceous mammals ate anything they could find. This helped them to survive the effects of the meteorite. After the dinosaurs died out, they were ready to take over the Earth. They are the ancestors of all the mammals we see in the world today.

Most of the ancient birds that were alive in the Cretaceous lived in trees. They died out when the forests died. Just like the mammals that survived this extinction event, the birds that survived were small and lived on the ground. They were happy to eat anything they could find.

Dinosaur adventure

Dinosaurs are the ancient ancestors of modern birds. Next time you spot a duck or a chicken, look closely. Compare the bird to the dinosaurs you've seen on your dinosaur adventure. Which features are the same? Which features are different?

Although the dinosaurs and pterosaurs died out, some other types of archosaurs survived. They include the ancestors of all the crocodiles and birds we see in the world today.

Wonderchicken

Let's get out of here! It's time we went home.

Asteriornis maastrichtensis is one of the earliest modern birds ever found, and is called the "Wonderchicken". Its ancestors were theropod dinosaurs. Birds like the Wonderchicken are the ancestors of today's ducks and chickens.

45

Glossary

ancestor	an animal from which another animal has evolved
ankylosaur	a group of bulky, armoured dinosaurs
archosaur	a group of reptiles that first emerged during the Triassic
bird	a winged animal that can typically fly
carnivore	an animal that only eats meat
climate	the weather in a certain area over a long period of time
continent	land that is grouped together
coprolite	fossilized dung
Cretaceous	a period of Earth's history that began 145 million years ago
dinosaur	a type of archosaur that first appeared on Earth around 240 million years ago
extinct	when a plant or animal no longer exists
fossil	special rocks that show the shapes of plants and animals that lived millions of years ago
frill	a hard extension on the back of some dinosaurs' heads, often used for defence
hadrosaur	dinosaurs that had skulls shaped like a duck's head with a bill
herbivore	an animal that eats plants
Jurassic	a period of Earth's history that began 201 million years ago
mammal	a warm-blooded animal that has a backbone and grows hair or fur
ocean	a large body of water
omnivore	an animal that eats plants and other animals
Pangaea	a huge continent that existed over 300 million years ago
Panthalassa	a huge ocean that existed over 300 million years ago
Permian	a period of Earth's history that began over 299 million years ago
predator	an animal that hunts and eats other animals
prey	an animal that is hunted and eaten by another animal
pterosaur	an archosaur with wings made of skin and muscle
raptor	a group of dinosaurs that were close relatives of the first birds on Earth
reptile	a cold-blooded animal that usually has scaly skin
sail	long spines connected by skin that grow out of a dinosaur's back
sauropod	a group of large plant-eating dinosaurs that had long tails and necks, and walked on four legs
sedimentary rock	a rock that is formed in layers when broken pieces of other rocks join together
serrated	a sharp, jagged edge
stegosaur	a group of dinosaurs with rows of bony plates and spikes along their backs and tails
therapsid	a reptile that lived in the Permian and could heat its own body
theropod	a dinosaur that usually used only two legs for walking, also known as 'beast-footed'
titanosaur	a group of gigantic sauropods and the largest land animals to have ever lived on Earth
Triassic	a period of Earth's history that began about 251 million years ago
tyrannosaur	a huge, meat-eating dinosaur with small arms, a large head and sharp teeth

Ankylosaurus • ang-KIGH-luh-SOR-us
Ankylosaurus magniventris

Yutyrannus • yoo-tigh-RA-nuhs
Yutyrannus huali

Spinosaurus • SPIGH-nuh-SOR-us
Spinosaurus aegyptiacus

Dilophosaurus • di-LOFF-oh-SOR-us
Dilophosaurus wetherilli

Giraffatitan • ji-RAF-ah-tigh-tan
Giraffatitan brancai